# Going Deeper and Doing More

DAG HEWARD-MILLS

*Parchment House*

Unless otherwise stated, all Scripture quotations are taken from the King James Version of the Bible.

**Going Deeper and Doing More**



First published by Parchment House 2022

Published by Parchment House 2022
1st Printing 2022

[77]Find out more about Dag Heward-Mills
Healing Jesus Campaign
Write to: evangelist@daghewardmills.org
Website: www.daghewardmills.org
Facebook: Dag Heward-Mills
Twitter: @EvangelistDag

ISBN: 978-1-64330-517-2

# *Contents*


1. Go Deeper into the Deep Things of God .......... 1
2. How God Takes You Deeper .......... 6
3. Go Deeper in Love and Do More .......... 16
4. Go Deeper in the Anointing and Do More .......... 21
5. Go Deeper and Win More Souls .......... 25
6. Go Deeper and Build more .......... 30
7. Go Deeper into Wisdom and Do More .......... 36
8. Go Deeper and be More Fruitful .......... 39
9. How to Go Deeper in Knowledge .......... 54
10. Go Deeper by the Art of Repetition .......... 64

## CHAPTER 1

# Go Deeper into the Deep Things of God

**But as it is written, Eye hath not seen, nor ear heard, neither have entered into the heart of man, the things which God hath prepared for them that love him. But God hath revealed them unto us by his Spirit: for the Spirit searcheth all things, yea, THE DEEP THINGS OF GOD.**

**1 Corinthians 2:9-10**

There are deep things of God. Do you want to enjoy the deeper things of God? I am sure you do and that is why you are reading this book. There are many advantages of going deeper in the things of God.

If you go deeper, you will do more!

If you go deeper in God, you will find yourself enjoying a much greater dimension of the Lord. What are some of the areas you can go deeper into?

1. **Go deeper into the Holy of Holies: You can go deeper into the Holy of Holies.**

> That's how everything was arranged in the holy tent. The priests entered it at regular times. They went into the outer room to do their work for God and others. BUT ONLY THE HIGH PRIEST WENT INTO THE INNER ROOM. He went in only once a year. He never entered without taking blood with him. He offered the blood for himself. He also offered it for the sins the people had committed because they didn't know any better.
>
> Hebrews 9:6-7 (NIRV)

The Holy of Holies is the inner chamber of God. That is the inner room where the holiest presence of God is found. You can stay outside the tabernacle where the masses gather. You can go deeper into the outer court of the tabernacle. You can go even deeper into the holy place. But you can go into the deepest realm of God that is called the Holy of Holies. In the old covenant, only the High Priest dared to venture into this innermost sanctum.

Today, there is a realm in God you can penetrate in which you experience the holiest of holies. What does it mean to experience the holiest of holies? It is to experience the presence of God in a real way. Normally, you and I are aware of the weather, the temperature, the humidity, the chair we are sitting on and the people that are around us; but there is a realm in God where you can feel His presence. It is time to start feeling more than the temperature and the humidity of the room you are in. When you start feeling his presence in a real way, you are entering into the Holy of Holies.

2. **Go deeper into the glory: so that you can enjoy God more. Moses was a man to go deeper and do more: Moses went deeper in God Himself.**

> And the Lord said unto Moses, I will do this thing also that thou hast spoken: for thou hast found grace in my sight, and I know thee by name. And he said, I BESEECH THEE, SHEW ME THY GLORY. And he said, I will make all my goodness pass before thee, and I will proclaim the name of the Lord before thee; and will be gracious to whom I will be gracious, and will shew mercy on whom I will shew mercy.
>
> Exodus 33:17-19

Moses sought to go deeper and experience the glory of God. "Show me thy glory" was his prayer.

When you go deeper, you will experience the glory of God. God does not reveal His glory to just anyone. Many really rich and prosperous people do not reveal or expose their true wealth and glory. Some people show off their riches and glory. Usually, that is a sign that there is not much else hidden away.

Truly wealthy people do not show off their wealth. For instance, Switzerland, a very small country, has one of the highest numbers of millionaires and billionaires in the world. Walking through Switzerland, you would hardly believe that there are so many millionaires and billionaires there. Switzerland, which has a low population of 8.5 million people has more millionaires than India with a population of 1.4 billion people. You would have to go deeper in Switzerland to understand how beautifully rich the people are and how much gold and wealth is in their country. God is like that! You would need to go deeper to see His glory, His beauty, His wealth, His splendour and His majesty.

Go deeper into the beauty of the Lord by dwelling in the house of the Lord. David was a man to go deeper and do more so that he could enjoy the beauty of the Lord. David wanted to dwell in the house of the Lord and not just to visit once a week. That is how to go deeper. Do not visit the house of the Lord once a week. Dwell in the house of the Lord and you will see His beauty and His glory.

> One thing have I desired of the Lord, that will I seek after; that I may dwell in the house of the Lord all the days of my life, to behold the beauty of the Lord, and to enquire in his temple.
>
> Psalm 27:4

**4. Go deeper into the power and glory: David was a man to go deeper so he could enjoy the power and glory of God**

> O GOD, THOU ART MY GOD; EARLY WILL I SEEK THEE: MY SOUL THIRSTETH FOR THEE, MY FLESH LONGETH FOR THEE IN A DRY AND THIRSTY LAND, WHERE NO WATER IS; TO SEE THY POWER AND THY GLORY, so as I have seen thee in the sanctuary. Because thy lovingkindness is better than life, my lips shall praise thee. Thus will I bless thee while I live: I will lift up my hands in thy name. My soul shall be satisfied as with marrow and fatness; and my mouth shall praise thee with joyful lips: When I remember thee upon my bed, and meditate on thee in the night watches. Because thou hast been my help, therefore in the shadow of thy wings will I rejoice. My soul followeth hard after thee: thy right hand upholdeth me. But those that seek my soul, to destroy it, shall go into the lower parts of the earth.
>
> Psalm 63:1-9

We need to go deeper in God if we want to see His power. Years ago, I was a teacher of the word of God. At a very young age, people began to enjoy my preaching. People would buy and listen to tapes that I preached. But I yearned to see the power of God. I wanted to go deeper so I could see His power and His glory in my life and ministry.

Do you have miracles in your ministry? Do you have large crusades? Are the sick brought to your meetings so that they receive healing? Is there a move of the Spirit in your church services?

Do people fall under the power of God when you minister to them? Do you have "words of knowledge" and "words of wisdom"? If your answer to any of these questions is No, then you need to seek after the power of God for your life and ministry.

You will seek after the power of God by going deeper. There is something more than the level you have attained in God. You can go deeper and do more. Going deeper will bring you to the power level of ministry. You will be like David whose flesh longed for God in a dry and thirsty land until he saw the power of God in his life.

CHAPTER 2

# How God Takes You Deeper

**Deep calleth unto deep...**

**Psalm 42:7**

## 1. GOD TAKES YOU DEEPER THROUGH YOUR HUNGER AND THIRST FOR MORE.

**Blessed are they which do hunger and thirst after righteousness: for they shall be filled.**

**Matthew 5:6**

Only those who have a thirst for more get to go deeper. Only a hunger and thirst for God can start you on a journey to go deeper. Without a hunger and a thirst, you can never get more of God. Blessed are they which do hunger and thirst after righteousness, for they shall be filled.

It is very difficult to get somebody to have a drink when he is not thirsty. There must be a thirst before there can be a drink. People who are not thirsty do not even ask for drinks. You cannot make people who are not thirsty drink deeply. They will even start begging you to stop forcing them to drink. They may start choking over your drink because they just cannot take any thing in. Notice how David was thirsty for more of God.

> O GOD, THOU ART MY GOD; EARLY WILL I SEEK THEE: MY SOUL THIRSTETH FOR THEE, MY FLESH LONGETH FOR THEE IN A DRY AND THIRSTY LAND, WHERE NO WATER IS; To see thy power and thy glory, so as I have seen thee in the sanctuary. Because thy lovingkindness is better than life, my lips shall praise thee. Thus will I bless thee while I live: I will lift up my hands in thy name. My soul shall be satisfied as with marrow and fatness; and my mouth shall praise thee with joyful lips: When I remember thee upon my bed, and meditate on thee in the night watches. Because thou hast been my help, therefore in the shadow of thy wings will I rejoice.
>
> Psalm 63:1-7

When a person experiences a great change in his spiritual life, it is usually because there was a change in the levels of desire and the levels of thirst for God. You must pray for people to have a desire and a thirst for God. That is when they will really change.

Apostle Paul knew that there would be no real ministry unless there was a desire. That was why he told Timothy to look for people who have a strong desire before making them bishops. Only a desire can take you on a journey to go deeper in God.

Pray for good desires from God! Desires for God and a thirst for God are used to direct people deeper into the will of God.

A desire is the almost magical prescription for you to go deeper. Without reading any special verses from the bible or receiving any special visions or dreams, desires will take you deeper into the will of God. God planted in woman the desire for man. This desire has caused the will of God to come to pass. Women naturally fulfil the will of God by desiring men and receiving the seed.

God knows that everything begins with a desire, a thirst, a longing and a passion. When he wants to bless you, He will bless you with a desire, a thirst, a longing and a passion.

Moses was blessed with a longing and a passion for God. That is why he cried, "Show me Your glory." Moses cried, "I beseech you!" Moses was virtually begging God to show him His glory.

> And the Lord said unto Moses, I will do this thing also that thou hast spoken: for thou hast found grace in my sight, and I know thee by name. AND HE SAID, I BESEECH THEE, SHEW ME THY GLORY. And he said, I will make all my goodness pass before thee, and I will proclaim the name of the Lord before thee; and will be gracious to whom I will be gracious, and will shew mercy on whom I will shew mercy.
>
> Exodus 33:17-19

**2. GOD TAKES YOU DEEPER BY CONVINCING YOU TO DO MORE THAN YOU DID AT THE BEGINNING.**

**To the angel of the church in Thyatira write: These are the words of the Son of God, whose eyes are like blazing fire and whose feet are like burnished bronze. I know your deeds, your love and faith, your service and perseverance, AND THAT YOU ARE NOW DOING MORE THAN YOU DID AT FIRST.**

**Revelation 2:18-19 (NIV)**

The church of Thyatira was recognized for doing more than they did at the beginning. If you won twenty souls in 1995, how come you are still winning twenty souls this year? Surely, a whole lot of things transpire as the years go by. Ships and planes are bigger than they were at first! Shops and malls are bigger than they have ever been! Why should churches not be bigger too? Why should you not do more than you did at the beginning? If you are doing less today, it should spur you on to do more.

What is your calling? What has God given you to do? You must do more and you must do better than you did at the beginning. Do not be satisfied with your results! Are you doing more than you did at the beginning?

## 3. GOD TAKES YOU DEEPER BY SHOWING YOU THAT GOD IS GOOD.

**And the Lord said unto Moses, I will do this thing also that thou hast spoken: for thou hast found grace in my sight, and I know thee by name. And he said, I beseech thee, shew me thy glory. And he said, I WILL MAKE ALL MY GOODNESS PASS BEFORE THEE, and I will proclaim the name of the Lord before thee; and will be gracious to whom I will be gracious, and will shew mercy on whom I will shew mercy.**

**Exodus 33:17-19**

God is a good God. You would not want to go deeper into God if He was not a good God.

Unless you think that someone is a good person, you would not want be close to him. You would not be attracted to someone who is not a good person.

A man thinks that a woman is a good person and that is why he is attracted to her. This is why God showed His goodness to Moses. He wanted Moses to be attracted to Him and come deeper.

I once knew someone who was trying to separate one of my workers from me. He kept on giving this person messages and information about me that made me look bad. Ultimately he was trying to separate this person from me. The devil works hard at his smear campaign to make ministers of the gospel look bad. Indeed, the devil works hard at his smear campaign to make God look bad.

That is the power of separation at work. Separation always occurs when someone is reported to be a bad person. That is why Satan is behind all forms of slander, defamation and calumny. He wants you to look bad so that people will not come near you.

The devil's aim is to make you see or think that God is a bad or unkind God. This is how he keeps people away from going deeper into God. When Satan approached Adam and Eve, he suggested that God was unkind by withholding the one important tree from them.

Satan told them: "God does not want you to have good things! God does not want you to be like a god and know the basic difference between good and evil. How unkind, how unreasonable and how wicked God is! Why would God keep such basic information from human beings? God does not want you to be able to protect yourself in this world. That is why He does not let you know the difference between good and evil." These are the words of the devil and the voice of separation.

I believe that God is good. It is my belief in His goodness that drew me to Him. It is my belief in His goodness that drew me to serve Him fulltime and all the time. I believe that God is so good that one day He will put a crown on my head and make me into royalty before Him.

I believe that God is so good that one day He will fill my arms with rewards upon rewards that will make every moment that I have served Him worth the while. What a good God we serve! Do not let the enemy deceive you about the goodness of God.

In your relationship with important people, do not let the devil fill your mind with thoughts that your boss, your father and your important person does not like you. Do not let the serpent envenomate you. Do not be poisoned against the very people whom you need to be close to. To separate you from your important people is one of the basic strategies of the devil.

## 4. GOD TAKES YOU DEEPER BY TEACHING YOU MERCY AND FORGIVENESS.

> And the Lord descended in the cloud, and stood with him there, and proclaimed the name of the Lord. And the Lord passed by before him, and proclaimed, THE LORD, THE LORD GOD, MERCIFUL AND GRACIOUS, LONGSUFFERING, AND ABUNDANT IN GOODNESS AND TRUTH, KEEPING MERCY FOR THOUSANDS, FORGIVING INIQUITY AND TRANSGRESSION AND SIN, and that will by no means clear the guilty; visiting the iniquity of the fathers upon the children, and upon the children's children, unto the third and to the fourth generation. And Moses made haste, and bowed his head toward the earth, and worshipped.
>
> Exodus 34:5-8

Going deeper into God will involve going deeper into mercy and forgiveness. When God takes you deeper into Him, He is taking you deeper into His mercy, grace and forgiveness. Today, God is embarking on a journey to draw you to Him. God is love. Love forgives. Love is gracious and kind and forgiving and merciful. The word mercy in the Old Testament is translated from the word "*Rechab*" which speaks of the womb.

You see, you are able to forgive someone that came out of your womb. God has a feeling towards you that mothers have for those that came out of their womb. There is a kindness, there is gentleness, there is favour, and there is graciousness that you have towards those who come out of your womb and belong to you.

In order to draw you closer to Himself, God will give you a reason to learn forgiveness. He will cause you to be hurt and offended so that you can learn to love and forgive. As you grow in love and forgiveness, you will be growing in the nature of God and you will come close to God.

Having to forgive people and truly overlook their mistakes is a great leap forward into the depths of God. God is love. As you get deeper into love and forgiveness, you will be getting deeper into God.

**5. GOD TAKES YOU DEEPER BY TEACHING YOU LONGSUFFERING.**

> And the Lord descended in the cloud, and stood with him there, and proclaimed the name of the Lord. AND THE LORD PASSED BY BEFORE HIM, AND PROCLAIMED, THE LORD, THE LORD GOD, MERCIFUL AND GRACIOUS, LONGSUFFERING, AND ABUNDANT IN GOODNESS AND TRUTH, Keeping mercy for thousands, forgiving iniquity and transgression and sin, and that will by no means clear the guilty; visiting the iniquity of the fathers upon the children, and upon the children's children, unto the third and to the fourth generation. And Moses made haste, and bowed his head toward the earth, and worshipped.
>
> Exodus 34:5-8

When God wanted to take Moses closer, He decided to show him His longsuffering. We must learn from Moses' experience with God. God drew Moses closer and showed him His glory. Moses saw the glory of God when he saw the longsuffering of God.

As you learn more about patience you are getting closer to the nature of God and can go deeper into him. God is a very patient God. He endures the wickedness of mankind as though he does not see what we are doing.

The world marches on and hundreds of years go by and it is as though God does not see the blasphemies of men. Human beings blaspheme and insult God every day. They say God does not exist! God listens to people insulting Him in their rooms, on television and on social media.

God suffers long and waits patiently. Patiently waiting is a divine characteristic! Your impatience reveals your pride. Your impatience reveals how close you are to satan. Your longsuffering reveals how close you are to God.

Allow yourself to learn the almighty lesson of patience. Have patience with God. He will avenge you of your enemies. God will strike down your foes and those who threaten your existence.

### 6. GOD TAKES YOU DEEPER BY SHOWING YOU ABOUT TRUTH.

**And the Lord descended in the cloud, and stood with him there, and proclaimed the name of the Lord. And the Lord passed by before him, and proclaimed, THE LORD, THE LORD GOD, MERCIFUL AND GRACIOUS, LONGSUFFERING, AND ABUNDANT IN GOODNESS AND TRUTH, Keeping mercy for thousands, forgiving iniquity and transgression and sin, and that will by no means clear the guilty; visiting the iniquity of the fathers upon the children, and upon the children's children, unto the third and to the fourth generation. And Moses made haste, and bowed his head toward the earth, and worshipped.**

**Exodus 34:5-8**

When God wanted to take Moses closer, He showed him the truth. We must learn from Moses' experience with God. God drew Moses closer and showed him His glory. Moses saw the glory of God when he saw how God was full of truth.

Remember that Jesus said, "I am the way, the truth and the life." Satan represents lies and deception. The more the deception, the more there are demons. Satan is a liar and a father of it.

I once met a brother who deceived his entire family and all his friends. His deceptions revealed how much demon activity was at work in his life. One person remarked about how easily this fellow told lies. Remember that liars will be cast into the lake of fire.

The deeper you are into truth, the deeper you are into God. God is truth and light. There is no darkness in him at all. Any form of deception or self-deception will keep you from God. God is light so the deeper you are into light, the deeper you are into God.

> **This then is the message which we have heard of him, and declare unto you, that God is light, and in him is no darkness at all.**
>
> **1 John 1:5**

## 7. GOD TOOK MOSES DEEPER BY SHOWING HIM HOW TO COMBINE MERCY WITH JUDGMENT.

> And the Lord descended in the cloud, and stood with him there, and proclaimed the name of the Lord. And the Lord passed by before him, and proclaimed, The Lord, The Lord God, merciful and gracious, longsuffering, and abundant in goodness and truth, KEEPING MERCY FOR THOUSANDS, FORGIVING INIQUITY AND TRANSGRESSION AND SIN, AND THAT WILL BY NO MEANS CLEAR THE GUILTY; visiting the iniquity of the fathers upon the children, and upon the children's children, unto the third and to the fourth generation. And Moses made haste, and bowed his head toward the earth, and worshipped.
>
> Exodus 34:5-8

God takes you deeper by showing you His judgments of people. Judgment requires God's mind and God's wisdom. Only deep people can understand or even fathom why God would punish generations of innocent people for their parents' sin.

God is able to show mercy and at the same time not clear the guilty. This is a deep and complex aspect of God's nature. If you can attain to combining the love and mercy of God with the judgment of God, you are close to God's heart.

If you can learn how to show forgiveness and at the same time, punish those who are guilty, you would have moved much closer to the Lord. Go deeper by learning these complex aspects of God!

## CHAPTER 3

# Go Deeper in Love and Do More

**That Christ may dwell in your hearts by faith; that ye, BEING ROOTED AND GROUNDED IN LOVE, MAY BE ABLE TO COMPREHEND WITH ALL SAINTS WHAT IS THE BREADTH, AND LENGTH, AND DEPTH, AND HEIGHT; And to know the love of Christ, which passeth knowledge, that ye might be filled with all the fulness of God.**

**Ephesians 3:17-19**

If you are rooted and grounded in love, you comprehend the length and depth and height. Going deeper in love opens you up to heights and depths that you have never known before.

What does this mean?

If you love your nursing job, you will go deeper and know the breadth and length and height and depth of nursing. If your nursing career is rooted in love for people, you will discover lengths and depths and heights of nursing that a person who does not have this love cannot know.

Most people do things without having a love for it. If you love being a doctor, you will discover the length and depth and height of it. You will go as far as you can go in studies, in research, in acquiring degrees, in acquiring knowledge and in acquiring experience. When I was in medical school, I had some classmates who really loved medicine. They were so excited to be training to become doctors. They did everything to know the length and depth and breadth of medicine. They even attended extra-curricular lectures.

I did not have that love for the medical course I was doing. I wanted to do the basic minimum and get away with it. Whenever there was a special lecturer from America or elsewhere I would not attend.

I was not rooted and grounded in love for the medical career. I loved God and the ministry more. That is where I went deeper.

When you are rooted and grounded in love for something, you start to look for the length and the breadth and the height and the depth of it.

1. Do more by loving more: Love God and you will go deeper. Love the Father more! When you love the Father which is in heaven you will try to obey Him. To Almighty God, love is obedience and obedience is love!

The more you love God, the more obedient you will be. If you have great love for the Father, you will search for the depth and length and height and breadth of obedience in God. You will seek to be the most obedient child of God just because of your love for God.

> **He that hath my commandments, and keepeth them, he it is that loveth me: and he that loveth me shall be loved of my Father, and I will love him, and will manifest myself to him.**
>
> **John 14:21**

2. Do more by obeying more: Philemon did more because of his obedience. Philemon did more because his obedience was more. Doing more is the sign that you are walking in obedience to God.

> **Yea, brother, let me have joy of thee in the Lord: refresh my bowels in the Lord. HAVING CONFIDENCE IN THY OBEDIENCE I WROTE UNTO THEE, KNOWING THAT THOU WILT ALSO DO MORE THAN I SAY. But withal prepare me also a lodging: for I trust that through your prayers I shall be given unto you.**
>
> **Philemon 1:20-22**

3. Do more by loving more: Love Jesus more! Peter was expected to do more than other disciples because he was expected to have more love for Jesus. Jesus expected him to feed the lambs just because of his love for Him. The more you love God, the more you will do.

**When they had finished eating, Jesus said to Simon Peter, "Simon son of John, DO YOU LOVE ME MORE THAN THESE?" "Yes, Lord," he said, "you know that I love you." Jesus said, "Feed my lambs."**

**John 21:15 (NIV)**

4. Do more by loving more: Love God, love the Holy Spirit more! You can do more when you have the *love of the Spirit.* Those who love the anointing are those who go into the length and breadth and height of the anointing. You will seek to understand the anointing and to follow it if you *love the Spirit.* You will go into the depths of the lives of anointed people because you *love the Spirit.* You will not criticize anointed people because you love the Spirit.

**And I am sure that, when I come unto you, I shall come in the fulness of the blessing of the gospel of Christ. Now I beseech you, brethren, for the Lord Jesus Christ's sake, AND FOR THE LOVE OF THE SPIRIT, that ye strive together with me in your prayers to God for me; That I may be delivered from them that do not believe in Judaea; and that my service which I have for Jerusalem may be accepted of the saints;**

**Romans 15:29-31**

5. Do more by loving people more: Do more because of love and forgiveness! It is important to love people if you are going to achieve more with people. When you love more, you will enter the length and breadth and depth and height of looking after people. You will not enter the length and depth and breadth and height of pastoral work until you do it out of love. No one can be a good pastor because of a good salary.

Good salaries cannot give you the motivation to go into the length and depth and breadth of caring for people.

**But I say unto you, Love your enemies, bless them that curse you, do good to them that hate you, and pray for them which despitefully use you, and persecute you; That ye may be the children of your Father which is in heaven: for he maketh his sun to rise on the evil and on the good, and sendeth rain on the just and on the unjust. For if ye love them which love you, what reward have ye? Do not even the publicans the same? AND IF YE SALUTE YOUR BRETHREN ONLY, WHAT DO YE MORE THAN OTHERS? do not even the publicans so? Be ye therefore perfect, even as your Father which is in heaven is perfect.**

**Matthew 5:44-48**

## CHAPTER 4

# Go Deeper in the Anointing and Do More

**Afterward he brought me again unto the door of the house; and, behold, waters issued out from under the threshold of the house eastward: for the forefront of the house stood toward the east, and the waters came down from under from the right side of the house, at the south side of the altar. Then brought he me out of the way of the gate northward, and led me about the way without unto the utter gate by the way that looketh eastward; and, behold, there ran out waters on the right side. And when the man that had the line in his hand went forth eastward, he measured a thousand cubits, and he brought me through the waters; THE WATERS WERE TO THE ANKLES. Again he measured a thousand, and brought me through the waters; THE WATERS WERE TO THE KNEES. Again he measured a thousand, and brought me through; THE WATERS WERE TO THE LOINS. Afterward he measured a thousand; and it was a river that I could not pass over: for the waters were risen, WATERS TO SWIM IN, a river that could not be passed over.**

**Ezekiel 47:1-5**

It is possible to go deeper in the anointing. The river described in Ezekiel is the river of God. It is a river of the anointing and a river of the power of the Holy Spirit. As you can see, it is possible to go deeper and deeper into a river.

The river gets deeper as you go in further. As you go deeper, the water rises from the ankles to the knees, then to the loins until it is so deep that you cannot stand. This river speaks of the anointing of the Holy Spirit. As you go deeper into the anointing of the Holy Spirit, your life will be controlled by the power of the Holy Spirit. Ezekiel's river is a message that says you can go deeper for the anointing!

## Going deeper for the Oil

In the natural, human beings dig very deep to get natural oil and gas. They realise that they must go vertically down otherwise they are not going to get much. Some of the oil wells are as deep as 10 to 15 km vertically deep below the earth. They are so deep and far and yet human beings have reached out to tap into the store of oil below the earth.

Can you imagine what is involved in digging a well that is 10 km deep? Can you imagine how far 10 km is horizontally?

These are fantastic feats of men seeking to go deeper to get more oil for the world. Why do you not think of going deeper to get more oil and anointing for the things of God?

Many of these wells are vertically drilled. I have listed, just four of the amazingly deep oil wells of the world.

1. *THE BERTHA ROGERS NO.1 ANARDARKO BASIN* IN OKLAHOMA USA IS 9.58 KM DEEP.

2. *THE BP DEEPWATER HORIZON TIBER FIELD* IN THE GULF OF MEXICO IN THE UNITED STATES OF AMERICA IS 10.66 KM DEEP.

3. *THE MAERSK DRILLING RAYA-1 BLOCK 14,* URUGUAY IS 3.4 KM DEEP AND *THE SAKHALIN O-14 CHAYVO FIELD* IN RUSSIA IS 14.9 KM DEEP.

4. *THE KOLA SUPERDEEP BOREHOLE*, THE DEEPEST HOLE EVER DUG REACHES APPROXIMATELY 7.5 MILES BELOW THE EARTH'S SURFACE (OR 12,262 KILOMETERS), A DEPTH THAT TOOK ABOUT 20 YEARS TO REACH. THE HOLE WAS INTENDED TO GO "AS DEEP AS POSSIBLE," WHICH RESEARCHES EXPECTED TO BE AROUND 14.5 KM.

It is time for you to go deeper and get the anointing that you need. What is it going to take for you to go deeper? You will have to spend the time and money to drill deeper and go further. You may be an anointed person but there is always more you can have.

You may have visions and dreams but there are always higher and greater visions than you can imagine. Thank God for your little hazy visions! You must be aware that people have had visions of Jesus Christ walking into a room tangibly and talking to them for two hours.

There is even deeper than that. People have had visions in which Jesus walked down the aisle into the church, in the full view of everyone. There are more and more fantastic and amazing possibilities in every field. Never think that you have arrived. You can go deeper.

There are deeper anointings of church growth. You can go deeper and get more. You can seek for greater anointings and you will have them. You will find out that your so-called mega church is actually a micro church. Go deeper and do more!

There are deeper evangelistic anointings. You will discover evangelists who speak to thousands of people and also teach the word of God. You will discover evangelists who win millions of souls and also build churches. Indeed, going deeper into the evangelistic anointing may lead you into dimensions of evangelism that you have never thought of. Go deeper and do more!

It is time for you to believe this fact! Anyone who is doing more is a deep person. He is wide and deep. He is indefinable and indefinite. Great men whom God uses are profound and deep in the things of God.

Your shallowness will never match up to their deepness. Until you become a deep person yourself, you will never be able to do more for God. It is time to drill even deeper!

# CHAPTER 5

# Go Deeper and Win More Souls

**And he entered into one of the ships, which was Simon's, and prayed him that he would thrust out a little from the land. And he sat down, and taught the people out of the ship. Now when he had left speaking, he said unto Simon, LAUNCH OUT INTO THE DEEP, AND LET DOWN YOUR NETS FOR A DRAUGHT.**

**Luke 5:3-4**

Although Jesus Christ was a carpenter, He knew that the disciples would have to go deeper if they wanted to catch more fish. By Jesus sending his disciples out into the deep, he forever established the principle of going deeper to do more. Go deeper so you can be a better fisher of men and win real souls.

Fishing in your bathtub is not going to yield much! Fishing in the stream by your house is not going to yield much! Fishing in deeper rivers and lakes is likely to get you something better. Fishing in the sea will get you even more.

It is time for your evangelistic ministry to be magnified. Evangelism is the fulfilment of all ministry. Apostle Paul encouraged Timothy to do the work of an evangelist because it would help him to convincingly accomplish his ministry.

In the King James Bible, Paul teaches, "Do the work of an evangelist so that you make full proof of your ministry." The word "full proof" speaks of entirely, convincingly and completely carrying your ministry to its conclusion.

> But watch thou in all things, endure afflictions, do the work of an evangelist, make full proof of thy ministry.
>
> 2 Timothy 4:5

Perhaps, you have wondered what God wants you to do next. How can you go deeper and do more? I am here to tell you to do what Paul said, Make full proof of your ministry by doing the work of an evangelist. Fulfil the ministry in every part by doing evangelism.

Carry through your ministry to the end and convincingly accomplish what God sent you into the world to do by doing the work of an evangelist. Do not let anyone deceive you to veer off into vain jangling and secular ideas.

Be more spiritual rather than more secular. Go deeper by becoming more spiritual rather than becoming more secular. Why should your ministry be likened to the CEO of a bank rather than to a shepherd in a field?

You do not go deeper in the ministry by using big words or quoting from biographies of secular men. Your quotations from these books do not mean that you have gone deeper. Listen to the simple words of Apostle Paul – go deeper in the ministry and convincingly and completely accomplish all that God has set before you by doing the work of an evangelist.

I am speaking to those who are pastors, prophets, apostles and teachers. I promise you that your apostolic ministry will go to higher heights when you embark on the work of evangelism. I am an apostle and I have built many churches. There is evidence of that. I can tell you that every ministry gift is mystically and convincingly accomplished as you do the work of an evangelist.

When apostles evangelize, the apostolic ministry is energized and empowered. When prophets evangelize they move a notch higher. The famous prophet Branham was involved in a lot of evangelism as a prophet. When pastors evangelize, their churches grow mystically.

> And let them sacrifice the sacrifices of thanksgiving, and declare his works with rejoicing. THEY THAT GO DOWN TO THE SEA IN SHIPS, THAT DO BUSINESS IN GREAT WATERS; THESE SEE THE WORKS OF THE LORD, and his wonders in the deep. For he commandeth, and raiseth the stormy wind, which lifteth up the waves thereof
>
> Psalm 107:22-25

It is time to go deeper into great waters. God is expecting to see you going further into great waters. You will do greater works and catch much bigger fish. Going deeper with evangelistic fishing gives rise to catches of much bigger souls and fish.

You will soon be catching whales and sharks as part of your ministry. There is no point in moaning over how small your ministry is. Go deeper and do more! When you go deeper, you will catch whales.

Instead of catching fish which can fit into your pocket, you will catch whales in which you can live. I see you catching blue whales in your ministry! Imagine catching a blue whale! Can you imagine what that represents in the spirit? Imagine catching a blue whale for the Lord!

> The blue whale is the largest animal ever to have lived on earth.
>
> The blue whale weighs as much as 30 elephants and three lorries!
>
> The blue whale is as long as a ten-story building!
>
> The blue whale is as long as three 60-seater buses together!
>
> The tongue of a blue whale alone can weigh as much as an elephant!
>
> The heart of a blue whale is as big as a car!
>
> The blue whale's heart will beat only two times in a minute!
>
> The heartbeat of a blue whale is so loud it can be heard 2 miles away!
>
> The blood vessels of a blue whale are so big that a man can swim through them!
>
> The calf (baby of a blue whale) is suckled in the water, drinking more than 600 litres of milk each day. The calf of a blue whale gains 90kg every day in its first year!
>
> The penis of a blue whale is10 feet long and one foot wide!
>
> The testis of a blue whale testis weighs 80 kg.
>
> The ejaculation of a blue whale produces several gallons per issue.

You must go deeper into evangelism and missions by following the example and the teaching of Jesus Christ. The master sent his servants to invite as many friends as possible. Obviously, these friends were living in the beautiful suburbs of their cities.

> Then said he unto him, A certain man made a great supper, and bade many: And sent his servant at supper time to say to them that were bidden, Come; for all things are now ready. And they all with one consent began to make excuse. The first said unto him, I have bought a piece of ground, and I must needs go and see it: I pray thee have me excused.
>
> And another said, I have bought five yoke of oxen, and I go to prove them: I pray thee have me excused. And another said, I have married a wife, and therefore I cannot come. So that servant came, and shewed his lord these things. Then the master of the house being angry said to his servant, GO OUT QUICKLY INTO THE STREETS AND LANES OF THE CITY, and bring in hither the poor, and the maimed, and the halt, and the blind. And the servant said, Lord, it is done as thou hast commanded, and yet there is room. And the lord said unto the servant, GO OUT INTO THE HIGHWAYS AND HEDGES, and compel them to come in, that my house may be filled. For I say unto you, that none of those men which were bidden shall taste of my supper.
>
> Luke 14:16-24

Here we learn a lesson of going deeper in evangelism and missions. The master now sent his servants to the streets and lanes of the city. Even after going to the streets and lanes of the city, there was still room at the party. The master then sent his servants to the highways. Even after the highways there was still room. The master now sent his servants to the hedges, the bushes and the forests.

By this story, Jesus teaches us to go further and further, deeper and deeper into the fields that are white unto the harvest. In your lifetime and my lifetime, we will never finish going into the mission fields. Do not think that you have finished anything. The world is too big for you to finish evangelizing and doing missions in your lifetime. We will be on this work till our very last breath.

## CHAPTER 6

# Go Deeper and Build more

**Whosoever cometh to me, and heareth my sayings, and doeth them, I will shew you to whom he is like: HE IS LIKE A MAN WHICH BUILT AN HOUSE, AND DIGGED DEEP, and laid the foundation on a rock: and when the flood arose, the stream beat vehemently upon that house, and could not shake it: for it was founded upon a rock. But he that heareth, and doeth not, is like a man that without a foundation built an house upon the earth; against which the stream did beat vehemently, and immediately it fell; and the ruin of that house was great.**

**Luke 6:47-49**

Jesus Christ was not an engineer but He knew that you had to dig deep in order to build a solid and great building. Do you want to build something for God? Yes, you do! You want to build His church? Yes, you do! You want to build a great church that will last through the ages and through the centuries until Jesus returns for His people.

## Go Deeper with a Mighty Foundation

Go deeper so you can build something great for God. Tall majestic structures are only possible by going deeper.

Let us build a great church for God.

Let us build a deep foundation of righteousness and biblical truths on which the great building God has given us to build will stand.

There are mighty foundations that you must not set aside.

The mighty foundation of salvation through the blood of Jesus Christ and through the cross of Jesus Christ must never be belittled or side-lined.

The mighty foundation of faithfulness and loyalty must be deeply rooted in the foundation

The mighty foundation of evangelism and outreach must be deeply rooted in the church we are building.

The mighty foundation of teaching the word of God and sticking to the word of God must be deeply rooted in the church we are building.

The mighty foundation of tithes and offerings as the source of financing for God's work must never be set aside.

The mighty foundation that God so loved that He gave His only begotten Son that whosoever believes in Him should not perish but have eternal life must never be set aside.

Going deeper with our foundations for the church will give rise to a greater and better building.

## Mighty Foundations for Mighty Buildings

The foundations of constructed buildings vary greatly according to what is being built. The principle is simple: the deeper and stronger the foundation, the greater and taller the building!

The foundation of a single storey building is about 200 mm deep.

The foundation of a 2-storey building is about 1.2 meters deep.

The foundation of a 3-storey building is 1.5 meters deep.

The foundation of the Empire State building in New York is 16.7m deep. The Empire State building itself is 443 meters tall.

The foundation of the 61-storey Sales force Tower in San Francisco is 94.5 meters. The Sales force Tower itself is 326 meters high.

The foundation of the 828 metre Burj Khalifa in Dubai is 50 metres.

The foundation of the 632 metre high Shanghai Tower in China is 31.4 metres deep.

The foundation of the Petronas Twin Towers in Malaysia is 114 metres deep. Each of the towers is 451.9 metre high.

The foundation of the 554 metre high Lotte World Tower in Seoul Korea is 30 metres deep.

## Protect the Mighty Foundations

At different seasons of the ministry, I noticed that foundational principles of the church were under attack.

I once noticed some of my pastors were seeking to remove the mighty foundations upon which our ministry had been built. The church is built on faithfulness, loyalty, lay people and the ministry, shepherding work, evangelism, tithing, the art of leadership and the anointing of the Holy Spirit.

"If the foundations be destroyed, what can the righteous do?" (Psalm 11:3)

## The Foundation of Lay Ministry

It is a foundation of our ministry that lay pastors work sacrificially and voluntarily without pay. We believe that God will reward and pay the lay pastors directly.

There arose some lay pastors who wanted to be paid salaries; but lay pastors are volunteers and are not to be paid.

They wanted lay pastors to be given money for petrol for their cars as well as money for maintenance of their car engines and money for spare parts. They claimed that their cars were suffering wear and tear from going to church every Sunday. These people also demanded financial hand-outs for musicians and choristers every week.

I had to fight off these people who wanted to destroy the lay ministry because they were attacking the deep foundation of lay ministry.

When such things arise, it is a direct threat to the spirit of the sacrificial volunteer and the layperson. By fighting a good fight, those who were attacking the foundations of the church were pushed back. When you are defending foundations you have to teach again the first principles of the oracles of God.

> **For when for the time ye ought to be teachers, ye have need that one teach you again which be the first principles of the oracles of God; and are become such as have need of milk, and not of strong meat.**
>
> **Hebrews 5:12**

## The Foundation of Loyalty

Loyalty and faithfulness without an independent spirit, without criticizing, without politics, without passivity, without deception and without rebellion against fathers, are foundations of our church. Then there arose some pastors who wanted to set aside the principles of loyalty. These characters engaged in murmuring, spreading tales, gossiping and spreading discontentment among the ranks of the leaders.

I had to rise up and drive these things away from the church. It is important to remove those who are disloyal from the ranks. It is better to have a few loyal people than many disloyal and double-minded fellows. It is important to oppose and to drive away anyone who seeks to destroy the foundations of your church and ministry.

## The Foundation of Tithing

Tithes and offerings are the main source of finance for the church. Tithing and offering are foundational practices of the church. If a pastor does not pay tithes, it means that his congregation will follow suit and not pay tithes. The pastor who does not pay tithes is setting a very bad example and promoting hypocrisy. Most pastors who do not pay tithes are backslidden. Such people have to be removed from the pastorate because they have a problem and must not be leaders of the flock. If a pastor does not pay tithes, he does not believe the word of God and must not be up there preaching it.

## The Foundation of Shepherding

I also experienced an attack on the shepherding foundation of the church. Raising up shepherds and practicing the work of shepherds is a foundation of our church and ministry. I noticed that some people who were called shepherds did not want to visit the sheep, pray for them and interact with them as they should. They wanted to turn the church into a Sunday church in which there is a superman in the pulpit doing all the work. Our ministry was built on shepherding which involves a lot of interaction with the sheep, a lot of outreaches, a lot of visitation and a lot of care.

## The Foundation of the Art of Leadership

The art of good leadership is also a foundation for our church and ministry. One day, I noticed a strong attack on the art of leadership. A leader is a builder. Without building, the church is left without a house and without a future. I began to have a lot of contention with pastors who did not want to build even though they had the money to do it. It was as though they were under a spell which prevented them from practically getting into the work of building the church. In that season, most of my conflicts were with pastors and bishops who were refusing to do the right thing and practically build the church.

It is important to protect the foundations on which a church and ministry are built. If the foundations are removed, what can the righteous do? (Psalm 11:3). Once the foundations of your church and ministry are removed, you will not be able to operate and bear much fruit in the Lord.

## CHAPTER 7

# Go Deeper into Wisdom and Do More

**O THE DEPTH OF THE RICHES BOTH OF THE WISDOM AND KNOWLEDGE OF GOD! How unsearchable are his judgments, and his ways past finding out! For who hath known the mind of the Lord? Or who hath been his counsellor?**

**Romans 11:33-34**

God's wisdom is unsearchable. God's wisdom is deep and wide. Wisdom is the source of riches and wealth. Wisdom is the source of long life. Wisdom is the source of silver and gold. Wisdom is the source of righteousness. Wisdom is the source of all the good things that we need and want in this life. "For wisdom is better than rubies; and all the things that may be desired are not to be compared to it. I wisdom dwell with prudence, and find out knowledge of witty inventions. The fear of the Lord is to hate evil: pride, and arrogancy, and the evil way, and the froward mouth, do I hate. Counsel is mine, and sound wisdom: I am understanding; I have strength. By me kings reign, and princes decree justice. By me princes rule, and nobles, even all the judges of the earth. I love them that love me; and those that seek me early shall find me. Riches and honour are with me; yea, durable riches and righteousness. My fruit is better than gold, yea, than fine gold; and my revenue than choice silver. I lead in the way of righteousness, in the midst of the paths of judgment: That I may cause those that love me to inherit substance; and I will fill their treasures. The Lord possessed me in the beginning of his way, before his works of old" (Proverbs 8:11-22).

So how come we are not enjoying such wealth and riches in our lives? Do we not have this wisdom? We do have this wisdom but we have not gone deep enough. If we do not go deep enough we will not strike the true riches of God's wisdom. Going deeper is the key to accessing true riches.

**Go deep for the gold!**

For instance, it is only when you go deeper in the gold mines that you discover real treasure. Gold deposits lie at a depth of between 1200 and 4500 metres. These gold deposits exist in marine sediments or metamorphic rock created deep in the earth's crust by high temperature and pressure.

[1]Six of the ten deepest mines in the world reside in a particular region of South Africa, while the remaining four are located in Canada and in the US. There was a time that South Africa produced as much as thirty per cent of the world's gold output.

*AngloGold Ashanti's Mponeng gold mine*, located south-west of Johannesburg in South Africa, is currently the deepest mine in the world. The operating depth at Mponeng mine ranged from between 3.16km to 3.84km below the surface by the end of 2018. Ongoing expansions are expected to extend the operating depth further to 4.27km.

*The TauTona Gold Mine*, located in the West Wits area of South Africa, is the second deepest pit in the world. *TauTona's* operational depth reaches up to 3.9km below the surface, and it has 800 km of tunnels and three shafts.

As you can see, it is only when you go very deep that you benefit from the rich deposits of gold that are right under us. A large part of the riches of South Africa came from the deep mines that were heavily loaded with gold.

If human beings can go as far as four kilometres beneath the surface and create as much as 800km of roads under the ground just to find some gold, it shows how deep we must go in order to tap into the unsearchable wisdom and riches of God.

You must study more! You must read more! And you must pray for the spirit of revelation even more so that you can tap into the unsearchable riches of the wisdom of God!

CHAPTER 8

# Go Deeper and be More Fruitful

**And he spake many things unto them in parables, saying, Behold, a sower went forth to sow; And when he sowed, some seeds fell by the way side, and the fowls came and devoured them up: Some fell upon stony places, where they had not much earth: and forthwith they sprung up, BECAUSE THEY HAD NO DEEPNESS OF EARTH: And when the sun was up, they were scorched; and because they had no root, they withered away.**

**Matthew 13:3-6**

# Fruitfulness Depends on Going Deeper

## 1. Go deeper by having deep roots.

**And it came to pass, as he sowed, some fell by the way side, and the fowls of the air came and devoured it up. And some fell on stony ground, where it had not much earth; and immediately it sprang up, BECAUSE IT HAD NO DEPTH OF EARTH:**

**But when the sun was up, it was scorched; and because it had no root, it withered away. And some fell among thorns, and the thorns grew up, and choked it, and it yielded no fruit. And other fell on good ground, and did yield fruit that sprang up and increased; and brought forth, some thirty, and some sixty, and some an hundred. And he said unto them, He that hath ears to hear, let him hear.**

**Mark 4:4-9**

As a tree, your roots must go deeper and get to the right depth. Fruitfulness is a product of your depth. In the parable of the Sower, Jesus made it clear that unless the seed went deep, it would not bear fruit. There are many things that do not grow until they go deeper.

You are a tree planted by the rivers of living water. You are the trees of righteousness, the planting of the Lord. As a tree, your roots must go deeper and get to the right depth.

As a tree of righteousness, it is time to go deeper so that you can do more and bear more fruit. It is not enough to be born again. You must go deeper and get to know the Lord.

**To appoint unto them that mourn in Zion, to give unto them beauty for ashes, the oil of joy for mourning, the garment of praise for the spirit of heaviness; THAT THEY MIGHT BE CALLED TREES OF**

**RIGHTEOUSNESS, the planting of the LORD, that he might be glorified.**

**Isaiah 61:3**

2. **Go deeper by giving yourself wholly.**

**Meditate upon these things; give thyself wholly to them; that thy profiting may appear to all.**

**1 Timothy 4:15**

Giving yourself wholly is the same as going deeper. Paul advised Timothy to give himself wholly to the ministry. Without giving himself wholly to the ministry, Timothy would not experience the fruitfulness that he wanted to see.

3. **Go deeper by pressing towards the mark of the high calling.**

Not as though I had already attained, either were already perfect: but I follow after, if that I may apprehend that for which also I am apprehended of Christ Jesus. Brethren, I count not myself to have apprehended: but this one thing I do, forgetting those things which are behind, and reaching forth unto those things which are before, I PRESS TOWARD THE MARK FOR THE PRIZE OF THE HIGH CALLING OF GOD IN CHRIST JESUS.

Let us therefore, as many as be perfect, be thus minded: and if in any thing ye be otherwise minded, God shall reveal even this unto you. Nevertheless, whereto we have already attained, let us walk by the same rule, let us mind the same thing. Brethren, be followers together of me, and mark them which walk so as ye have us for an ensample.

Philippians 3:12-17

Giving yourself wholly is the same as pressing towards the mark of the high calling. Apostle Paul tried to go deeper. Even though he had written half of the New Testament, he wanted to go deeper and do more. It is time for you to go deeper by pressing towards the mark.

**4. Go deeper by getting understanding.**

> In Gibeon the Lord appeared to Solomon in a dream by night: and God said, Ask what I shall give thee. And Solomon said, Thou hast shewed unto thy servant David my father great mercy, according as he walked before thee in truth, and in righteousness, and in uprightness of heart with thee; and thou hast kept for him this great kindness, that thou hast given him a son to sit on his throne, as it is this day. And now, O Lord my God, thou hast made thy servant king instead of David my father: and I am but a little child: I know not how to go out or come in. And thy servant is in the midst of thy people which thou hast chosen, a great people, that cannot be numbered nor counted for multitude. GIVE THEREFORE THY SERVANT AN UNDERSTANDING HEART TO JUDGE THY PEOPLE, THAT I MAY DISCERN BETWEEN GOOD AND BAD: FOR WHO IS ABLE TO JUDGE THIS THY SO GREAT A PEOPLE?
>
> 1 Kings 3:5-9

Solomon had been granted the divine favour of being anointed as the king. When God appeared to him, he wanted to go deeper into his calling of being a king and a leader. He wanted wisdom and understanding and knowledge so that he would be the best leader possible.

It is important to desire to go deeper as a leader. Many people in leadership positions are terrible leaders. The evidence of their terrible and fatally deficient leadership is the state of the nations that they lead.

Each group of incompetent leaders blames the last group of incompetent leaders for their current failures. Most people in these leadership positions accomplish nothing and rather give speeches and excuses for their failings.

It is important to pray like Solomon prayed otherwise your opportunity to lead will be littered with misadventures and self inflicted calamities of leadership.

The ruins, the poverty, the joblessness, the corruption, the crime, the confusion, the despair, the deception and the outrageous daylight robbery by leaders is evidence of them being incapable of doing the job.

If you were put in charge of a huge ship that had one thousand containers on board and asked to steer it from a port in West Africa to Singapore I do not think you would know how to do it. Leadership is like that. Many leaders are like newly appointed captains of a ship who do not know how to turn on the engine or switch on the lights of a ship.

If someone does not know how to put on the engine or the light on the ship, how will he know how to steer it out of the harbour and into the open waters without crashing into other ships? How would he know the way to Singapore? How would he know the difference between south, west and east? Would he know if there was fuel in the ship? Would he even know how many people were on board?

There is an anointing for leadership! There is a spirit of leadership. You can acquire that spirit of leadership. You can go deeper. You can get the anointing of leadership! Arise and press into the leadership anointing by studying and reading all that you can until the spirit of leadership is upon you.

> So the Lord said to Moses, "Take Joshua son of Nun, a man in whom is THE SPIRIT OF LEADERSHIP, and lay your hand on him. Have him stand before Eleazar the priest and the entire assembly and commission him in their

presence. Give him some of your authority so the whole Israelite community will obey him.

Numbers 27:18-20 (NIV)

5. **Go deeper into healing.**

**For from the least of them even unto the greatest of them every one is given to covetousness; and from the prophet even unto the priest every one dealeth falsely. THEY HAVE HEALED ALSO THE HURT OF THE DAUGHTER OF MY PEOPLE SLIGHTLY, SAYING, PEACE, PEACE; WHEN THERE IS NO PEACE. Were they ashamed when they had committed abomination? Nay, they were not at all ashamed, neither could they blush: therefore they shall fall among them that fall: at the time that I visit them they shall be cast down, saith the Lord.**

**Jeremiah 6:13-15**

God was angry with the prophet and the priest because they healed the problems only slightly. We can go deeper and bear more fruit in the lives of our church members. Many pastors do not go deep enough and do not engage the lives of the church members. They have very shallow relationships and do not know the real problems of the people. God is expecting shepherds to bear much more fruit by going deeper and solving the hurts of the people in a much deeper way.

**Woe be unto the pastors that destroy and scatter the sheep of my pasture! saith the Lord. Therefore thus saith the Lord God of Israel against the pastors that feed my people; Ye have scattered my flock, and driven them away, and have not visited them: behold, I will visit upon you the evil of your doings, saith the Lord.**

**Jeremiah 23:1-2**

Shepherds must do more to solve problems. Go deeper into solving problems and bringing healing to people. It is important for shepherds to help to neutralize the curses that are working in the lives of the sheep. Most of the problems of our church members are because of activated curses. Curses are the deep and underlying causes of all our problems. Curses go deep. They start from Adam, Eve and Noah. Unfortunately, many shepherds do not go deep enough. God is angry with his shepherds because they do not go deep enough into the problems of the sheep.

**6. Go deeper by implementing the laws of loyalty and disloyalty.**

> And he began to speak unto them by parables. A certain man planted a vineyard, and set an hedge about it, and digged a place for the winefat, and built a tower, and let it out to husbandmen, and went into a far country. And at the season he sent to the husbandmen a servant, that he might receive from the husbandmen of the fruit of the vineyard. And they caught him, and beat him, and sent him away empty. And again he sent unto them another servant; and at him they cast stones, and wounded him in the head, and sent him away shamefully handled. And again he sent another; and him they killed, and many others; beating some, and killing some. Having yet therefore one son, his wellbeloved, he sent him also last unto them, saying, they will reverence my son. But those husbandmen said among themselves, this is the heir; come, let us kill him, and the inheritance shall be ours.' And they took him, and killed him, and cast him out of the vineyard. WHAT SHALL THEREFORE THE LORD OF THE VINEYARD DO? HE WILL COME AND DESTROY THE HUSBANDMEN, AND WILL GIVE THE VINEYARD UNTO OTHERS.
>
> Mark 12:1-9

Go deeper by implementing the laws of loyalty. Actively remove disloyal, wicked and ungrateful people. After removing one disloyal person, you may need to continue pruning until all forms of disloyalty, wickedness and treachery are removed. There are some people who actually honour disloyal people and elevate them. You must implement the principles of loyalty and disloyalty. It is not good enough to just read about it.

One day, I had to deal with a disloyal person who was criticizing me and destabilizing the church. I dealt with him by casting out the scorner so that strife would cease.

If you are going to benefit from the teaching on loyalty, you need to be persistent in casting out scorners. You will need to implement the teachings on loyalty and disloyalty. You will need to go deeper in the art of detecting traitors, antagonists and anarchists. An anarchist is someone who destabilizes a government. Anarchists within a church destabilize the leadership within the church. Cast out the scorner and contention shall cease! (Proverbs 22:10)

**7. Go deeper into science and witty inventions.**

> **I wisdom dwell with prudence, and find out knowledge of witty inventions.**
>
> **Proverbs 8:12**

Going deeper by believing in technology and witty inventions. Go deeper by practically using technology and witty inventions to advance your ministry. Many spiritual people do not believe in technology. Solomon promoted witty inventions. Solomon liked and used witty inventions!

Unless you go deeper, you will not come by real knowledge that matters. There are people who read my books but because they do not go deeper they do not really benefit from them. All medical advances were as a result of hard searching and persistent seeking for revelation until important facts were discovered. Let me share with you a number of medical revelations that came by going deeper into medical research.

### Going deeper produced vaccines in 1796

[1]It is difficult to pinpoint when vaccines became an accepted practice, mostly because the journey to discovery was long and complicated. Beginning with an attempt by Edward Jenner in

1796 to use inoculations to tame the infamous smallpox virus, the usefulness and popularity of vaccines grew very quickly. Throughout the 1800s and early 1900s, various vaccinations were created to combat some of the world's deadliest diseases, including smallpox, rabies, tuberculosis, and cholera.[1] [2]Over the course of 200 years, one of the deadliest diseases known to man – the small pox – was wiped off the face of the earth. Today, vaccines continue to save millions of lives each year - including jabs that protect against the corona virus and that can help prevent some cancers.[2]

## Going deeper produced Anaesthesia in 1846

[3]Before the first use of a general anaesthetic in the mid-19th century, surgery was undertaken only as a last resort, with several patients opting for death rather than enduring the excruciating ordeal. Although there were countless earlier experiments with anaesthesia dating as far back to 4000 BC – William T. G. Morton made history in 1846 when he successfully used ether as an anaesthetic during surgery. Soon after, a faster-acting substance called chloroform became widely used, but was considered high-risk after several fatalities were reported. Over the 150 years since, safer anaesthetics have been developed, allowing millions of life-saving, painless operations to take place.[3]

## Going deeper led to the discovery of germs in 1861

Before the 'germ' theory came about, the widely believed theory was that disease was caused by 'spontaneous generation'. In other words, physicians of the time thought that disease could appear out of thin air, rather than being air-borne or transferred via skin-to-skin contact. [4]In 1861, French microbiologist Louis Pasteur proved through a simple experiment that infectious disease was a result of an invasion of specific microscopic organisms - also known as pathogens - into living hosts. This new understanding marked a significant turning point in how diseases were treated, controlled and prevented, helping to prevent devastating epidemics that were responsible for thousands of deaths every year, such as the plague, dysentery and typhoid fever.[4]

## Going deeper led to the discovery of Medical imaging in 1895

[5]The first medical imaging machines were X-rays. The X-ray, a form of electromagnetic radiation, was 'accidentally' invented in 1895 by German physicist Wilhelm Conrad Röntgen when experimenting with electrical currents through glass cathode-ray tubes. The discovery transformed medicine overnight and by the following year, Glasgow hospital opened the world's very first radiology department.[5]

Ultrasound, although originally discovered many years before, began being used for medical diagnosis in 1955. This medical imaging device uses high frequency sound waves to create a digital image, and was no less than ground-breaking in terms of detecting pre-natal conditions and other pelvic and abdominal abnormalities. In 1967, the computed tomography (CT) scanner was created, which uses X-ray detectors and computers to diagnose many different types of disease, and has become a fundamental diagnostic tool in modern medicine.

The next major medical imaging technology was discovered in 1973 when Paul Lauterbur produced the first magnetic resonance image (MRI). The nuclear magnetic resonance data creates detailed images within the body and is a crucial tool in detecting life-threatening conditions including tumours, cysts, damage to the brain and spinal cord and some heart and liver problems.

## Going deeper led to the discovery of Penicillin in 1928

[6]Alexander Fleming's penicillin, the world's first antibiotic, completely revolutionised the war against deadly bacteria. Famously, the Scottish biologist accidentally discovered the anti-bacterial 'mould' in a petri dish in 1928. However, Fleming's incredible findings were not properly recognised[6] [7]until the 1940s, when they began being mass-produced by American drug companies for use in World War II. Two other scientists were

responsible for the mass distribution of penicillin, Australian Howard Florey and Nazi-Germany refugee Ernst Chain, and their development of the substance ended up saving millions of future lives. Unfortunately, over the years certain bacterium have become increasingly resistant to antibiotics, leading to a world-wide crisis that calls for the pharmaceutical industry to develop new anti-bacterial treatments as soon as possible.[7]

## Going deeper led to Organ transplants in 1954

[8]In December 1954, the first successful kidney transplant was carried out by Dr Joseph Murray and Dr David Hume in Boston, USA. Despite many previous attempts in history, this was the first instance where the recipient of an organ transplant survived the operation. The turning point came when various technical issues were overcome, such as vascular anastomosis (the connection between two blood vessels), placement of the kidney and immune response. In 1963, the first lung transplant was carried out, followed by a pancreas/kidney in 1966, and liver and heart in 1967. Aside from saving thousands of lives in the years following, transplant procedures have also become increasingly innovative and complex, with doctors successfully completing the first "hand" transplant in 1998 and full-face transplant in 2010![8]

## Going deeper produced the Birth Control Pill

9Arguably, few developments have had as profound a social impact as the introduction of the birth control pill -- though its path to widespread use has been a rocky one.

Although the Federal Drug Administration approved contraception as safe in the early 1960s, it only became legal for married couples in 1965 and for unmarried couples in 1972.

But because of the Pill, countless women have been given control over their own fertility -- a concept that created a social revolution.

"Thinking about how it has transformed women's lives, in terms of family planning and the entry of women into the work force, its impact has been significant indeed," Baker said. "It was the first-ever lifestyle drug. It's not treating a disease, but it was making life better for women."[9]

## Going deeper produced safe childbirth

[10]Up until the middle of the 20th century in the United States, childbirth was considered to be the most feared part of a woman's life.

"Go into any old graveyard, and you always see a number of women who died in their 20s," Baker said. "That was in a large part due to childbirth."

With the advent of techniques in anaesthesia, caesarean section, and forceps delivery, the chances of a successful have pregnancy improved, at least in developed countries. Unfortunately, many resource-poor societies around the world still lag behind in this arena.[10]

## Going deeper exposed the risks of smoking in 1950

[11]People sensed that smoking was bad for some time before research supported these assumptions. For instance, Henry Ford decried smoking as immoral, and a generation of Americans believed that it could stunt growth. But two landmark case-control studies published in JAMA and the BMJ in 1950 triggered substantial interest in the risks and harms of smoking. Further research was followed by a drop in the prevalence of smoking for the first time, much to the chagrin of Big Tobacco, which was more than willing to fight dirty – particularly through the use of false advertising campaigns—in order to retain market share. Fortunately, as you may have noticed, smoking has now hit an all-time low among US adults.[11]

## Going deeper led to the discovery of antipsychotics in 1952

[12]Before the discovery of antipsychotics and other psychotropics, asylums of yore housed stigmatized, dangerous,

and mostly hopeless patients. Some of these patients received psychoanalysis, but most didn't. Instead, these patients were treated as prisoners.

By the 1940s, university researchers and drug manufacturers started exploring psychopharmacology and developing new compounds to treat psychiatric illness. By 1926, for instance, acetylcholine was understood to be a neurotransmitter. By 1937, antihistamines were identified, followed in 1943 by lysergic acid diethylamide (LSD). Furthermore, insulin coma therapy, electroconvulsive therapy, and leucotomy (ie prefrontal lobotomy), as well as sedatives including bromides, barbiturates, and paraldehyde, were being used to treat those with mental illness.

In 1950, chemist Paul Charpentier synthesized the drug 4560 RP, later called chlorpromazine, which is a member of the phenothiazine group of antihistamines. Based on the work of various luminaries, by 1954, chlorpromazine had been administered in double-blind trials in Canada, the United Kingdom, and the United States. However, psychoanalysts refused to accept the drug as a substitute for analytic psychotherapy. Nevertheless, the drug's effects were undeniable and, starting in 1956, the number of inmates in UK asylums dropped substantially, with antipsychotics and antidepressants subsequently becoming very popular.

"Without the discovery of drugs such as chlorpromazine we might still have the miserable confinements … a world of desperate remedies," wrote psychiatrist Trevor Turner, Homerton Hospital, London, United Kingdom, in an article published in BMJ. "Then the attendant's role was akin to a zookeeper's: feeding, scrubbing, and forcibly treating hundreds of 'demented' patients. The psychiatric workforce was largely cut off from surgical and physician colleagues, was of poor quality, and was readily mocked."[12]

### Going deeper led to the discovery of DNA in 1953

[13]As late as 1952, geneticists didn't know how DNA worked.

All of this changed with the 1953 discovery of the double helix by James Watson, PhD, and Francis Crick, PhD. Their discovery of DNA's structure was rooted in Gregor Mendel's theory on the principles of single gene inheritance in 1866, as well as Sir Archibald Garrod's elucidation of the inheritance pattern of alkaptonuria in 1923.

Drs. Watson and Crick, as well as Maurice Wilkins, PhD, were honoured with the Nobel Prize for Physiology or Medicine in 1962 for their discovery. But in the eyes of many, the prestige of this award will be forever tinged by sexism. In addition to Dr. Wilkins, Rosalind Franklin, PhD, helped produce x-ray diffraction images instrumental to the deduction of Drs. Watson and Crick that DNA is a three-dimensional helix. These images were shared with Drs. Crick and Watson without her permission, and she wasn't credited in any way.[13]

**Going deeper led to the use of Blood Transfusions in 1901**

[14] You only need to read a book set in the 1800s or earlier to know that, through history, women often died in childbirth. One of the most common reasons for that was uncontrolled bleeding after delivery.

James Blundell, a British obstetrician, knew that transfusing blood into these women could save them. He also knew that others had been experimenting with transfusions for almost 200 years, often with fatal results, mostly because of the practice of using animal blood.

After successful experiments transfusing blood from one animal of the same species to another, Blundell made his first human attempt in 1818 on a woman who was haemorrhaging after childbirth. With her husband as a donor, he transfused 4 ounces of blood into the woman.

She survived, but not all of Blundell's subsequent patients were so fortunate. Although Blundell was the first to understand that human blood needed to be used on other humans, no one yet knew that blood came in different types - and that a transfusion with the wrong type would lead to immune rejection and, often, death.

Transfusions remained a dicey affair until 1901 when an Austrian doctor, Karl Landsteiner, discovered the different blood groups and which ones could be safely mixed with others.

Continuing research by others gave doctors the ability to bank blood, separate it into such components as plasma and screen for blood-borne pathogens. Today, about 15 million transfusions take place in the United States each year. [14]

As you can see, all these medical revelations have revolutionized our lives. They came from those who wanted to go deeper and do more.

CHAPTER 9

# How to Go Deeper in Knowledge

**And beside this, giving all diligence, ADD to your faith virtue; and to virtue KNOWLEDGE;**

**2 Peter 1:5**

## 1. Go deeper in knowledge by Seeking and searching:

You must go deeper in knowledge by seeking and searching for knowledge like the Bereans. The Bereans were described as noble or high in rank because they sought for knowledge. Today, many Christians do not spend time studying and researching like the Bereans. It is important to search and find out things for yourself. God will raise your rank when you search the scriptures yourself.

> And the brethren immediately sent away Paul and Silas by night unto Berea: who coming thither went into the synagogue of the Jews. These were more noble than those in Thessalonica, in that they received the word with all readiness of mind, AND SEARCHED THE SCRIPTURES DAILY, WHETHER THOSE THINGS WERE SO.
>
> Acts 17:10-11

Josiah, the king of Israel had to search the scriptures for himself. He was amazed at what he found. He made covenants to walk after God and to keep His commandments. What a transformation that came over the life of the king when he decided to search the scriptures for himself!

> And the king sent, and they gathered unto him all the elders of Judah and of Jerusalem. And the king went up into the house of the Lord, and all the men of Judah and all the inhabitants of Jerusalem with him, and the priests, and the prophets, and all the people, both small and great: and HE READ IN THEIR EARS ALL THE WORDS OF THE BOOK OF THE COVENANT WHICH WAS FOUND IN THE HOUSE OF THE LORD. And THE KING STOOD BY A PILLAR, AND MADE A COVENANT BEFORE THE LORD, TO WALK AFTER THE LORD, and to keep his commandments and his testimonies and his statutes with all their heart and all their soul, to perform the words of this covenant that were written in this book. And all the people stood to the covenant.
>
> 2 Kings 23:1-3

Josiah went deeper by reading and searching through the book of the law himself. Books are an obvious source of knowledge. Many people who gain expertise in a particular field put it in writing. These books can be a source of finding solutions to anything. It is important to read all you can about the topic you are interested in, whether in the form of books, articles or magazines, in order to gain in-depth knowledge.

**2. Go deeper by loving the truth:**

> **And with all deceivableness of unrighteousness in them that perish; because they received not the love of the truth, that they might be saved. And for this cause God shall send them strong delusion, that they should believe a lie:**
>
> **2 Thessalonians 2:10-11**

The scripture above tells us that the deceivableness of the enemy works because they received not *the love of the truth.*

It is important to come to the place where you love the truth. People who love the truth are protected from deceptions. The only way to be protected from delusions is to be devoted to finding out the truth and to be devoted to accepting the truth, no matter what it is.

The worst thing that the devil can do to you is to deceive you. Satan is in this world to deceive and fool everyone until they are destroyed. When the world discovers that it has been fooled by the devil into thinking that there is no God, they will be in great shock. When the world discovers that it has been fooled into ignoring God and not worshipping Him, they will kick themselves in disbelief. Deception is satan's most wicked ploy. Satan is out to fool you and to make a fool of you.

Decide that you will accept the truth no matter how difficult it is. Decide that you will accept the truth even if it goes against you. Decide that you will accept the truth even if it is not in your favour. Your passionate love for the truth will protect you from satan's deceptions.

**3. Go deeper by studying the wisdom in Jesus:**

**For I would that ye knew what great conflict I have for you, and for them at Laodicea, and for as many as have not seen my face in the flesh; That their hearts might be comforted, being knit together in love, and unto all riches of the full assurance of understanding, to the acknowledgement of the mystery of God, and of the Father, and OF CHRIST; IN WHOM ARE HID ALL THE TREASURES OF WISDOM AND KNOWLEDGE.**

**Colossians 2:1-3**

**But of him are ye in Christ Jesus, WHO OF GOD IS MADE UNTO US WISDOM, and righteousness, and sanctification, and redemption: That, according as it is written, He that glorieth, let him glory in the Lord.**

**1 Corinthians 1:30-31**

In the scripture above, Jesus Christ is made wisdom to us. Jesus Christ is your wisdom.

Study Jesus Christ and you will be studying wisdom and knowledge. Jesus is wisdom. Knowing Jesus and all about Jesus will give you wisdom and knowledge.

Study Jesus' life and history. Studying Jesus as a person who can be touched, observed and looked into, will give you tremendous light and life.

Through studying, I have found Matthew, Mark, Luke and John to be the most revealing and enlightening books of the Bible. If I had to cut out all the books of the bible and preserve just four of them, I would preserve Matthew, Mark, Luke and John. These four books reveal the life and the teachings of Jesus Christ. Jesus Christ is my wisdom. Studying Jesus and what he went through is a prophecy of what I must go through. Looking at Jesus will reveal to me what I must do next.

Jesus Christ is made unto me wisdom. In Him are hid all the treasures of wisdom and knowledge (Colossians 2:3). Look closely at Jesus. Look upon His life. Try to touch Him and feel Him. He is your wisdom. He is your guide!

> **That which was from the beginning, WHICH WE HAVE HEARD, WHICH WE HAVE SEEN WITH OUR EYES, WHICH WE HAVE LOOKED UPON, and our hands have handled, of the Word of life; (For the life was manifested, and we have seen it, and bear witness, and shew unto you that eternal life, which was with the Father, and was manifested unto us;) That which we have seen and heard declare we unto you, that ye also may have fellowship with us: and truly our fellowship is with the Father, and with his Son Jesus Christ.**
>
> **1 John 1:1-3**

Jesus said many things that are so profound that no twenty-eight or twenty-nine-year-old would ever know. Jesus had not lived long enough to know the heartfelt problems of strangers, the sick the naked and those in prison. Jesus said "When saw we thee a stranger, and took thee in? Or naked, and clothed thee? Or when saw we thee sick, or in prison, and came unto thee?" (Matthew 25:38-39) These difficulties are things that you find out with the passage of time and with the broadest of experiences.

Jesus Christ is indeed the wisdom of God. His words are ultimate words. His words are profound words. His wisdom is not human wisdom. His life and experiences are full of nuggets of wisdom for you and I.

The wisdom of Jesus Christ is revealed in the things that he did as well as the things that he taught. "The former treatise have I made, O Theophilus, of all that Jesus began BOTH TO DO AND TEACH," (Acts 1:1)

The books of Matthew, Mark, Luke and John reveal both what Jesus did as well as what He taught. The red-letter part in certain editions of the Bible is what He taught and the black parts are what He did.

**4. Go deeper by studying people:**

> **Take my yoke upon you, and LEARN OF ME; for I am meek and lowly in heart: and ye shall find rest unto your souls. For my yoke is easy, and my burden is light.**
>
> **Matthew 11:29-30**

Another way to go deeper in knowledge is to study people. The scripture says, "Learn of me."

Study people! Learn of me! If you can learn of Jesus, you can learn of anyone else. People are knowledge and wisdom banks. You can learn of them! People are the biggest knowledge banks. From a very early age, we have always learned by observing other people. Whichever field you want to gain knowledge in, you will always find people who are experienced and have comprehensive knowledge in it. You can make use of their accomplishments, mistakes, experiences and know-how. You should associate yourself with people who are experts in the field that you want to gain knowledge in and study them carefully.

It is important to study not only what a person says, but also what a person does. That is what he means when he says, "Learn of me." "Learn of me" means, learn my ways, learn my habits, learn my moods, learn my leadership, learn about my decisions, learn about my friends, learn about my wealth, learn about my poverty, learn about my spirituality. There are many things to learn from someone. This is why we read biographies. You read a biography because you can learn of someone. You can learn from his mistakes. You can learn from his successes and his triumphs.

**5. Go deeper by experimentation:**

> **That seeing they may see, and not perceive; and hearing they may hear, and not understand; lest at any time they should be converted, and their sins should be forgiven them.**
>
> **Mark 4:12**

God has given you eyes to see and ears to hear that you may learn from the various experiences that you have. There are certain things you cannot learn unless you try them out. There are some people who quench every new idea that comes up. You must learn to identify such people and not share your new ideas with them. God is a God who does new things. Do not be averse to new things.

> BEHOLD, I WILL DO A NEW THING; now it shall spring forth; shall ye not know it? I will even make a way in the wilderness, and rivers in the desert.
>
> Isaiah 43:19

One day I was playing golf with Yonggi Cho. I asked him how I could avoid making great mistakes in the ministry. He smiled at me and said, "There is no way to do that because you learn by failing." He said that every time you try something and you fail, you learn a big lesson. That helps you to learn a lot and keep pressing on.

Indeed, you learn by failing. Many great discoveries were accidental. There are some things you will never know until you try them out. Indeed, you get to learn a lot through experimentation with new things. Indeed, you learn very quickly through experimentation. If your experiment fails, do not get discouraged. Remember, failure can often be a stepping-stone to success. Also, you must be ready to change your mind once things do not work out. Allow God to speak to you and lead you through the things you discover accidentally. Actually, in the secular world, many of the great inventions and discoveries we enjoy today were accidental discoveries.

Let us look at a few accidental discoveries:

[1]1. Penicillin was discovered accidentally.

One of the biggest medicinal breakthroughs in history came about entirely by accident. Sir Alexander Fleming interrupted his experimentation with the influenza virus for a two week holiday and when he returned he found that a mould had started to grow which deterred the virus. Penicillin was born and is now used to treat everything from acne to pneumonia.

2. Viagra was discovered accidentally.

Originally aiming to develop a treatment for angina, Pfizer found their new prototype drug was igniting erections in men during the tests. A quick PR campaign with Pele later and Viagra was born.

3. Plastic was discovered accidentally.

A little over a century ago, the Belgian scientist, Leo Baekeland, accidentally made plastic. Originally naming the mixture of formaldehyde and phenol after himself, Bakelite, the scientist accidentally revolutionised pretty much everything in production and manufacturing.

4. The Microwave was discovered accidentally.

As WWII was drawing to a close, engineer, Percy Spencer, was attempting to develop energy sources for radar equipment. Whilst that didn't work out, Spencer did realise the chocolate bar in his pocket had melted, and went on to test his accidental invention by making popcorn.

5. Vaseline was discovered accidentally.

The fantastically named Robert Chesebrough was so enamoured when he accidentally discovered Vaseline that he started using it for all kinds of purposes – even eating a spoonful every day. Chesebrough was originally on the hunt for oil when the petroleum jelly made itself known.

6. Strikeable Match was discovered accidentally.

At the end of an amazing chain of events, English pharmacist, John Walker, accidentally got a lump of his fun new mixture of antimony sulphide and potassium chlorate on the end of his mixing stick. Naturally, he tried to scratch it off and it burst into flames – a terrifying but incredible breakthrough.

7. Gunpowder was discovered accidentally.

Most of these accidental discoveries came about as a result of scientists trying to create something similar to the final product. However, 9th century Chinese alchemists couldn't have been further from success when they accidentally developed gunpowder. They were trying to find an elixir for eternal life.

8. Corn Flakes was discovered accidentally.

The daily breakfast of millions of people all around the world, Corn Flakes were invented when Will Keith Kellogg accidentally left some wheat on the boil. The world's most famous cereal was created and a dynasty was born.

9. Anaesthesia was discovered accidentally.

During the early 1800s, ether and nitrous oxide were both widely abused by folks attending 'laughing parties'. When the laughter died down, someone pointed out the substance could help mask pain, and anaesthesia was born.[1]

**6. Go deeper by observation and meditation.**

> **I went by the field of the slothful, and by the vineyard of the man void of understanding; And, lo, it was all grown over with thorns, and nettles had covered the face thereof, and the stone wall thereof was broken down. Then I saw, and considered it well: I looked upon it, and received instruction. Yet a little sleep, a little slumber, a little folding of the hands to sleep: So shall thy poverty come as one that travelleth; and thy want as an armed man.**
>
> **Proverbs 24:30-34**

Passing by the field of the slothful and by the vineyard of a man void of understanding is like going to the university all over again. There is so much to learn from this man's field and vineyard. By this man's field, God is teaching you the secret of prosperity. By this overgrown field, God is teaching you about the causes of intractable poverty. By this overgrown field, God is showing you the power of decay, deterioration and decadence. By observing the slothful man, God is showing you what he does not want you to be like. God is showing you whom he does not want you to follow.

A lot of the things you will learn in your life will not come by formal lectures in a classroom. Many of the important lessons will be learnt out of the classroom. You will have to learn them by observation, by listening carefully and by meditating on all that you see. Today, I know many things that I did not know when I was in school. I have learnt so much by being in the ministry. I have never been to bible school. I have never had the privilege of sitting in a bible school lecture. I have had to learn many things in the ministry by observation, by experience and by thinking deeply about what I see.

God will allow you to see certain things at close quarters. He wants you to learn from what you see in your family. He wants you to learn from what you see in your parents. He wants you to learn from what you see in ministers ahead of you. He wants you to learn from tragedies that happen around you. He wants you to learn from successful people around you. He wants you to learn from problems that arise nearby as well as crises that you hear of from afar.

---

1-1 | 10 Accidental Scientific Discoveries and Breakthroughs| Retrieved from: *https://www.mynewlab.com/blog/accidental-scientific-discoveries-and-breakthroughs/*

# CHAPTER 10

# Go Deeper by the Art of Repetition

**...TO WRITE THE SAME THINGS TO YOU, to me indeed is not grievous, but for you it is safe.**
**Philippians 3:1**

The art of repetition is the art of doing something frequently, repeatedly, twice, once more, again, twofold often, anew, over again, afresh, many times over, time and again, time after time, year after year, every day, every hour, every moment.

**1. Go deeper by repetitive reading.**

> **Finally, my brethren, rejoice in the Lord. TO WRITE THE SAME THINGS TO YOU, TO ME INDEED IS NOT GRIEVOUS, but for you it is safe. Beware of dogs, beware of evil workers, beware of the concision. For we are the circumcision, which worship God in the spirit, and rejoice in Christ Jesus, and have no confidence in the flesh.**
>
> **Philippians 3:1-3**

Go into the riches of wisdom and knowledge by repetitive reading. You will never know what is in a book until you have read it at least nine times. It is important to keep reading the same books over and over until you glean and harvest the knowledge and wisdom that is in them. My favourite books are still my favourite books.

I still glean knowledge and harvest knowledge from the books I have been reading for the last sixteen years. It seems that certain books and writers are anointed for you. God will use them over and over again to illuminate your life. It is amazing how the same book can release fresh light and revelation, even though you have read it before.

**2. Go deeper by reading wider.**

> **And when this epistle is read among you, cause that it be read also in the church of the Laodiceans; and that ye LIKEWISE READ THE EPISTLE FROM LAODICEA.**
>
> **Colossians 4:16**

Go deeper into the riches of wisdom and knowledge by wider reading. There are people who only read from one author. It is important to read widely! Paul asked the Colossians to read the letter for the Laodiceans. He also wanted the Laodiceans to read the letter to the Colossians.

I have read parts of the journal of John Wesley as well as several different biographies of John Wesley. As you know, John Wesley belongs to the Methodists and I am not a Methodist. However, I believe that I must read things that belong to the Methodists to make me broader and deeper. If I only read the books that are meant for Charismatics I would be narrow minded and limited in knowledge.

I can go deeper by reading books written to other sectors of the church. Paul asked that the Laodiceans should read the Colossians' letter. It is a pity that we cannot find the Laodiceans' letter. What a difference it would have made to the church! This little instruction by Paul teaches us how we must go deeper by reading from other places.

**3. Go deeper by repeated warnings.**

> **My son, despise not the chastening of the Lord; neither be weary of his correction: For whom the Lord loveth he correcteth; even as a father the son in whom he delighteth.**
>
> **Proverbs 3:11-12**

> **THIS IS THE THIRD TIME I AM COMING TO YOU. In the mouth of two or three witnesses shall every word be established. I told you before, and foretell you, as if I were present, the second time; and being absent now I write to them which heretofore have sinned, and to all other, that, if I come again, I will not spare:**
>
> **2 Corinthians 13:1-2**

Correction must also be repeated. Many times we are not aware of the mistakes that we are making in life and ministry. Sometimes reprimanding someone is not enough. Sometimes one meeting is not enough to let a correction come through. Sometimes it takes one year and four months of repetitive correction for a message to sink through. Go deeper and do more by repeatedly correcting what must be corrected. As Paul said, this is the third time I am coming to you. He was ready to rebuke them for the third time on the same issue.

There are some people who do not want their mistakes to be mentioned again. But the scripture teaches that he that hateth reproof shall die. "Correction is grievous unto him that forsaketh the way: and he that hateth reproof shall die" (Proverbs 15:10).

Such people are irritated and angered that their mistakes should be mentioned at a meeting. They hate to be used as examples of anything that is slightly negative.

They say things like, "In this system, nothing is ever forgotten. There is no love and forgiveness in this system."

They say things like, "Your problem will be spread around and told to every one in the system." They say things like, "The system will never forgive you. You will be written about in a book or sang about in a song."

They say things like, "You will be swatted like a fly if you tell the truth."

Indeed, many people absolutely hate correction. As Jeremiah said, these are a people who do not receive correction.

> But thou shalt say unto them, this is a nation that obeyeth not the voice of the Lord their God, nor receiveth correction: truth is perished, and is cut off from their mouth.
>
> Jeremiah 7:28

**4. Go deeper by repetitive prayers.**

> **Saying, There was in a city a judge, which feared not God, neither regarded man: And there was a widow in that city; and she came unto him, saying, avenge me of mine adversary. And he would not for a while: but**

**afterward he said within himself, Though I fear not God, nor regard man; Yet because this widow troubleth me, I will avenge her, lest BY HER CONTINUAL COMING SHE WEARY ME. And the Lord said, hear what the unjust judge saith.**

**Luke 18:2-6**

Repeatedly coming to God in prayer is not a bad thing. Do not be deceived by anyone who says you should not repeat your prayers. If you pray often, you will by all means repeat your prayers. I am always praying for the Holy Spirit. I am always praying for the Spirit of wisdom and revelation. I believe I will continue praying for these Spirits even if it is repetitive.

Jesus commended this lady for her coming continually to the judge. Keep coming continually to the Judge of the whole earth. God will avenge you for your repeated coming. Repeatedly coming in prayer makes you go deeper.

**5. Go deeper by repetitively seeking God's direction.**

**And the Philistines yet again spread themselves abroad in the valley. THEREFORE DAVID ENQUIRED AGAIN OF GOD; and God said unto him, Go not up after them; turn away from them, and come upon them over against the mulberry trees. And it shall be, when thou shalt hear a sound of going in the tops of the mulberry trees, that then thou shalt go out to battle: for God is gone forth before thee to smite the host of the Philistines. David therefore did as God commanded him: and they smote the host of the Philistines from Gibeon even to Gazer. And the fame of David went out into all lands; and the Lord brought the fear of him upon all nations.**

**1 Chronicles 14:13-17**

The will of God is something that is important to pray for repeatedly. Why is this? Circumstances change every day. Deception looms all around every day. Demons that we cannot see hover around, seeking to deceive, to kill and to destroy.

When Jesus was in the Garden of Gethsemane he prayed repeatedly about the will of God. For three hours he agonized that the will of God should be done. Why would Jesus have to pray about the will of God?

If Jesus did not pray about the will of God, the will of God would not have been done. That is why He prayed about it. It is important for you to pray continuously about the will of God until it comes to pass. Do not be fooled into thinking that you do not need to pray about the will of God in your life. Go deeper into the will of God by constantly seeking the Father's direction.

**6. Go deeper by repeated visitation:**

> **THIS IS THE THIRD TIME I AM COMING TO YOU. In the mouth of two or three witnesses shall every word be established. I told you before, and foretell you, as if I were present, the second time; and being absent now I write to them which heretofore have sinned, and to all other, that, if I come again, I will not spare:**
>
> **2 Corinthians 13:1-2**

Every shepherd must go deeper by doing more of the same thing. Repeated visiting and repeated evangelism will take you deeper and make you accomplish more. Paul visited the Corinthians for the third time. His three visits to the Corinthians made him the greatest spiritual leader of all time to come out of Corinth.

Do not be afraid of visiting the same person three times! Do not be afraid of visiting the same church three times. Do not be afraid of having a crusade at the same venue three times! Go deeper and do more. Visit more and accomplish more as a shepherd.

**7. Go deeper by repeated visits.**

> **Neither went I up to Jerusalem to them which were apostles before me; but I went into Arabia, and RETURNED AGAIN UNTO DAMASCUS. Then after**

**three years I went up to Jerusalem to see Peter, and abode with him fifteen days.**

**Galatians 1:17-18**

Only repeated visits to Israel will make you understand the Holy Land. Repetition of your visits to memorable places in your journey with God are important to establish in you certain truths and revelations that God has imparted to you.

Over the years, I have been to certain places which have spiritual significance to me. Notice that Paul was converted at Damascus. Notice how Paul went back to Damascus on other occasions. Many years ago, I prayed on a street and asked God to make me fruitful. I always remember that street where I walked and prayed and sought the Lord. I really wanted God to make me a fruitful Christian. I can understand why Paul would go back to Damascus, the place where he met Christ.

And Saul, yet breathing out threatenings and slaughter against the disciples of the Lord, went unto the high priest, And desired of him letters to Damascus to the synagogues, that if he found any of this way, whether they were men or women, he might bring them bound unto Jerusalem. AND AS HE JOURNEYED, HE CAME NEAR DAMASCUS: AND SUDDENLY THERE SHINED ROUND ABOUT HIM A LIGHT FROM HEAVEN: And he fell to the earth, and heard a voice saying unto him, Saul, Saul, why persecutest thou me? And he said, who art thou, Lord? And the Lord said, I am Jesus whom thou persecutest: it is hard for thee to kick against the pricks.

Acts 9:1-5

Paul returned to Damascus a number of times. He probably refreshed his soul in the place where he met the Lord Jesus Christ. It is important to go back to the places where God touched you. God will speak to you again in the same place!

**8. Go deeper by repeated giving.**

> **Now ye Philippians know also, that in the beginning of the gospel, when I departed from Macedonia, no church communicated with me as concerning giving and receiving, but ye only. For even in Thessalonica YE SENT ONCE AND AGAIN UNTO MY NECESSITY. Not because I desire a gift: but I desire fruit that may abound to your account. But I have all, and abound: I am full, having received of Epaphroditus the things which were sent from you, an odour of a sweet smell, a sacrifice acceptable, wellpleasing to God. But my God shall supply all your need according to his riches in glory by Christ Jesus.**
>
> **Philippians 4:15-19**

Go deeper by giving and giving again. To whom much is given, much is required. Do not be surprised that you are being asked to give again. Do not be surprised that you would be asked to give the same thing again. Paul said that the Macedonians had sent supplies to him once and had sent again.

God is requiring you to go deeper and do more in every way, including your finances.

## Conclusion

God is going to help you to go deeper and to do more!

It is important that you consider these few words sufficient to advise you as you serve the Lord!

To the making of many books there is no end! Please consider these few words deeply and you will bear much fruit in the Lord.

# References

## Chapter 7

Excerpts from:

The top ten deepest mines in the world| Retrieved from: *https://www.mining-technology.com/features/feature-top-ten-deepest-mines-world-south-africa/.*

## Chapter 8

Excerpts from:

1-1Top 15 Medical Inventions That Changed the World |SurgMedia. Retrieved from: *https://surgmedia.com/top-15-medical-inventions-changed-world/*

2-2Medical terms that have changed over time. Retrieved from: *https://registrybit.com/another-name-bwo/61be26-medical-terms-that-have-changed-over-time*

3-3Medicine. Retrieved from: *https://norgrovehomeschool.blogspot.com/2021/10/medicine.html*

4-4Medical History timeline: Retrieved from: | *Timetoast timelines. https://www.timetoast.com/timelines/medical-history-056c3e54-cf75-49b1-9f33-8d35c17f5981*

5-5Medicine. Retrieved from: *https://norgrovehomeschool.blogspot.com/2021/10/medicine.html*

6-6Medicine. Retrieved from: *https://norgrovehomeschool.blogspot.com/2021/10/medicine.html*

7-7Top 15 Medical Inventions That Changed the World | SurgMedia. Retrieved from: *https://surgmedia.com/top-15-medical-inventions-changed-world/*

8-8The Commonwealth of Health -Massachusetts's Great Medical Retrieved from: *https://pioneerinstitute.org/covid/covid-edu/eduresources/the-commonwealth-of-health-massachusettss-great-medical-innovations-15-resources-for-high-school-students/*

9-9 Ten Health Advances That Changed the World - ABC News. Retrieved from: *https://abcnews.go.com/Health/TenWays/story?id=3605442&page=1*

10-10 Ten Health Advances That Changed the World - ABC News. Retrieved from: *https://abcnews.go.com/Health/TenWays/story?id=3605442&page=1*

11-11: Greatest medical discoveries in the past 100 years. Retrieved from: *https://www.healingwell.com/community/default.aspx?f=35&m=4148038*

12-12: Greatest medical discoveries in the past 100 years. Retrieved from: *https://www.healingwell.com/community/default.aspx?f=35&m=4148038*

13-13 Greatest medical discoveries in the past 100 years. Retrieved from: *https://www.healingwell.com/community/default.aspx?f=35&m=4148038*

14-14 10 Breakthrough Moments in Medicine | Discover Magazine. Retrieved from: *https://www.discovermagazine.com/health/10-breakthrough-moments-in-medicine*

**Chapter 9**

1-1 10 Accidental Scientific Discoveries and Breakthroughs. Retrievied from: *https://www.mynewlab.com/blog/accidental-scientific-discoveries-and-breakthroughs/*